10   17 16 15
ISBN 978-3-88117-730-6
Design: Niels Bonnemeier
Cover illustration: Christiane Leesker
Translation: John Lovegrove
Editing: Monika Römer, Roger Cope
© 2006 Verlag W. Hölker GmbH, Münster
www.hoelker-verlag.de

Barbara Rias-Bucher

The little
German
Cookbook

Hölker Verlag

Content

If not stated otherwise,
the recipes are for 4 servings.

Foreword

A little German cookery book – with a great variety of regional recipes but without any pretence of being complete. The regions correspond more or less to the sixteen states which make up the Federal Republic. Their cookery traditions are so strong that the typical dishes are common knowledge and have withstood fast-food and multi-cultural influences. We Germans have loved beef broth and lentil soup, meat balls and *Wurst* salad, sour beef and pork roasts, Cheese *Spätzle* and potato pancakes, *Rote Grütze* and apple cake for generations. And for this reason these dishes are to be found in this book. Of course culinary tourist attractions such as *Labskaus* and liver dumpling soup, onion cake and *Handkäs mit Musik* should not be omitted although these dishes have remained regional specialities. Then there are classic examples of common German cooking such as *Königsberger Klopse* and creamy goulash, trout *"Müllerin"* and *Leipziger Allerlei*, asparagus and *Pichelsteiner*. More complex dishes such as *Maultaschen* are described as well as simple ham noodles and apple pancakes. But please do not just concentrate on the main recipes; regional specialities are also to be found in the additional cooking tips. All in all there are approximately 60 recipes which represent culinary pleasure in Germany.

Naturally I had to forgo many dishes as the ingredients are not available in other countries: *Pinkelwürste* for the traditional Bremen curly cale soup, hop shoots for the Bavarian salad or elder for the Hamburg *Fliederbeer* soup. For many dishes German cooks no longer use self-made ingredients. In the Palatinate, Bavaria and Thuringia one usually buys ready-made high quality dough to prepare the potato dumplings to go with the traditional Sunday roast. One leaves the preparation of the Palatinate Saumagen, well-known outside of Germany, to a restaurant one trusts.

Other dishes do not require a recipe: *Strammer Max* from Berlin for example is simply a slice of buttered bread covered with diced ham and a fried egg.

I believe that German cooking is reasonably simple. Perhaps because the refinement of French cuisine and genial simplicity to be found in Italy or the opulent elegance of Viennese cooking are missing. Perhaps we still feel the seasons despite an abundance of groceries and foodstuffs: winter tastes in Germany different from summer, in spring we hunger for asparagus and herbs and the autumn smells of plum cake. The characteristic "mother's home cooking" might seem silly and petit bourgeois but it reflects the heart of the matter: our eating habits in the centre of Europe have transformed all external influences into a down-to-earth, often solid and more often excellent plain fare. For this reason German dishes are so popular far afield.

I hope you will enjoy reading this book and cooking and savouring the dishes.

Soups and stews

Potato soup with sausages

This soup is one of the most important German dishes. To make a full meal of it sausages are added to this Berlin recipe. In Baden one enjoys it by adding fried diced bacon bits. In Hessen the soup has a creamy consistence and is served with fried onions. The Bavarians pour it over thin slices of fried rye bread whereas in the Palatinate and Franconia one eats it with a nice piece of freshly cooled-off plum cake (ref.: recipe for *Zwetschgendatschi* – Plum cake, p. 74).

1 large onion, 700 g floury potatoes,
1 large carrot, 1 parsley root, 100 g celeriac,
1 leek, 2 tbsp oil, 1/2 tbsp dried marjoram,
1 tsp caraway seeds, 1 1/2 l meat stock,
4 Frankfurter sausages,
salt, freshly ground pepper,
2 tsp each of chopped parsley and chives

Peel or prepare the onion, potatoes, carrot, parsley root and celeriac and finely dice. Cut the prepared leek into small pieces.
Heat the oil in a large saucepan and stir fry onion and marjoram at low heat. Add the vegetables. Pour in the stock and bring to the boil. Simmer the soup at moderately high heat for approx. 15 minutes. Then slightly mash the soft vegetables. Heat up the whole or sliced sausages in the soup but do not boil. Season to taste with salt and pepper and serve with the chopped parsley and chives.

Beef broth with vegetables

1 small carrot, 100 g celeriac,
1 small leek, 1 onion,
1 bunch of parsley,
1 bay leaf, salt,
500 g lean boiling beef,
1 1/2 l stock

Peel or prepare the vegetables and halve the onion. Rinse the parsley. Place all ingredients together with the bay leaf and a tbsp of salt in a large saucepan. Add the rinsed meat and stock and bring gently to boil covered in the saucepan. Continue to simmer for about 2 hours until the meat is tender. Remove the meat and dice. Sieve the stock and dispose of the vegetables, parsley and bay leaf. Skim off any fat if necessary.

The stock can now be used for any of the following soups:

Variation: For vegetable soup – finely slice 400 g carrots, green beans, courgettes, celery sticks and boil for 10 minutes in the stock. Add 150 g cauliflower buds and the diced meat and simmer for a further 10 minutes. Serve sprinkled with parsley.

Variation: For the Palatinate vegetable soup boil a diced potatoe with the other vegetables. Melt 2 tbsp of butter and golden fry 2 tbsp of breadcrumbs. Mix into the soup when serving.

Variation: For the semolina dumpling soup boil up the stock in a large saucepan. Mix 40 g soft butter, 1 large egg, salt, a pinch of nutmeg and 1 tbsp chopped parsley in a bowl. Stir in about 100 g semolina. Form small dumplings with the help of 2 teaspoons and add to the boiling stock. Always keep the spoons moist to avoid sticking. Leave the dumplings to simmer gently in a half covered pan for about 20 minutes. Then remove from the heat and leave to stand for a further 5 minutes. Serve the soup with chopped chives.

Variation: For pancake soup roll a freshly fried pancake, cut into thin strips and place in a soup plate. Pour over the hot stock and serve with chive rings.

Variation: For the Berlin noodle soup boil up 400 g ribbon noodles in the stock. Shortly before the noodles are al dente add the diced meat and 1–2 handfuls of coarsely chopped lovage leaves. Stir well and season to taste with pepper and salt. Serve immediately.

Sliced green bean soup

750 g fresh green beans,
1 bunch of savory, 1 onion, 2 tbsp oil,
1 tbsp mashed potato powder,
1 1/4 l vegetable or meat stock,
2 tbsp sour cream, 1–2 tsp lemon juice,
salt, freshly ground pepper

Rinse, top and tail the beans and slice diagonally in small pieces. Rinse and dry the savory. Pluck off several leaves and put aside. Peel the onion, dice finely and gently fry in hot oil. Add the beans and the savory and short fry together with the onions. Sprinkle the mashed potato powder over the beans, stir, pour in the stock and bring to the boil. Cover the soup and leave to boil for about 15 minutes. By then the beans should be tender. Remove the savory. Add the sour cream with the remaining savory leaves. Season the soup to taste with lemon juice, salt and pepper.

Lentil soup

1 onion, 1 small carrot, 100 g celeriac,
1 small leek, 2 tbsp oil, 150 g lentils,
1 piece of smoked bacon (200 g),
1 tbsp vegetable stock extract, 2 potatoes, preferably
waxy, salt, freshly ground white pepper,
2–4 tbsp red wine vinegar, 1 tbsp chopped parsley

Peal or prepare and finely chop onion, carrot, celeriac
and leek. Fry these ingredients in a saucepan with hot
oil until the onions become transparent. Add the lentils
and stir several times. Place the bacon in the pan, pour
in 1 1/2 l of water and bring to the boil. Add the stock
extract. Leave the soup to simmer covered at moderately high heat for 30 minutes.
In the meantime peal and dice the potatoes. Add to the
soup, return to the boil and cook for 15–20 minutes
until the potatoes are soft-boiled. Remove the bacon,
dice and add to the soup again. Season to taste with
salt, pepper and the chopped parsley.

 One can transform this typical German lentil soup
into a Swabian speciality: Prepare as above but
using 250 g lentils and only 1 l of water.
Make a soft dough from 250 g flour, salt, 4 eggs
and a little water and prepare *Spätzle* as described
in the recipe for *Allgäuer Kässpatzn*, (p. 59). Turn
the *Spätzle* in hot butter. Heat up 8 Frankfurter sausages and serve the lentils, sausages and *Spätzle* in
soup plates.

Liver dumpling soup

For 6 portions
4 slightly stale wheat bread rolls,
1/4 l warm milk, 50 g streaky smoked bacon,
1 small onion, 1 tsp oil, 2 tbsp chopped parsley,
150 g finely sliced beef liver, 75 g minced beef, 2 eggs,
1 tsp dried marjoram, 1 tsp untreated lemon peel,
freshly grated nutmeg, salt, freshly ground pepper,
1–2 tbsp bread crumbs (optional),
1 1/2 l of meat stock

Thinly slice the bread rolls and place in a bowl. Pour in the milk and allow to soak. Finely dice the bacon and the pealed onion and stir fry at low heat until transparent. Add half of the parsley. Then mix the contents of the pan and all other ingredients, apart from the bread-crumbs, rest of the parsley and the stock. Knead everything into a homogenous dough. Add more bread-crumbs if neccessary. With wet hands mould 6 dumplings, place in the stock and bring to the boil. Leave the dumplings to simmer for a maximum of 30 minutes, do not let them boil. Serve the soup with dumplings in pre-warmed plates and sprinkle with chopped parsley.

This soup is eaten in the Palatinate and Bavaria together with freshly made liver sausages, black pudding and boiled pork. As a substantial main meal it is served with mashed potatoes and sauerkraut (ref.: Recipe for Schweinswürstel with sauerkraut, p. 21).

Löffelerbsen – Pea soup

For 6 portions
500 g dried yellow peas (without seed coat),
approx. 750 g lightly salted pork (cheek or knuckle),
2 large carrots, 1 small celeriac, 500 g potatoes,
2 leeks, 300 g fresh pork sausages, salt,
freshly ground white pepper

Put the peas in a saucepan and cover with water. Put a lid on the pan and bring the peas to the boil. Leave to simmer at low heat for approx. 1 1/2 hours until soft. Boil the salted pork in a separate pot, half covered, at low heat for 1 hour. In the meantime peel and dice the carrots, celeriac and potatoes. Prepare the leeks, halve them lengthwise and thinly slice them. When the meat is cooked add the vegetables, bring shortly to the boil and leave to simmer for 20 minutes. Add the sausages, remove from the heat and allow to draw for 10 minutes.

Remove the meat from the stock and cut in slices, if necessary remove from the bone. Place the meat together with the sausages on a pre-warmed plate.

Mash the peas and add the meat stock together with the vegetables. Season to taste with salt and pepper, serve in a bowl with the meat and sausages.

 This traditional Berlin dish is usually eaten with rye bread and spiced gherkins. A simple variation is to cook the peas to a thick soup, add the potatoes and warm up large sliced Frankfurters.

Pichelsteiner meat

This square meal from the Bavarian Forest is famous since the year 1874: every year on the last weekend in July the small town of Regen celebrates the Pichelsteiner meat. Apart from the stew and beer in abundance there is a torchlight procession and a concert.

For 6 Portions
250 g boiling beef
(ask your butcher for advice),
250 g boneless shoulder of pork,
250 g boneless shoulder of lamb,
2 onions, 750 g potatoes, preferably floury,
400 g celeriac, 4 large carrots,
3 large parsnips or parsley roots,
1 large leek, 3 tbsp oil, salt,
freshly ground black pepper,
2 tbsp of clarified butter,
1/2 l meat stock,
3–4 tbsp chopped parsley,
3–4 tbsp chopped chives

Wash and dry the pieces of meat and dice in 2 cm pieces. Peel and dice the onions. Peel the potatoes, celeriac, carrots, parsnips and parsley roots and cut in fingerwidth slices. Clean the leeks and cut diagonally in equal slices. First sauté the meat, then the onions and vegetables separately and remove from the pan.

Now place the ingredients back in layers in the roasting tin, spicing each layer with salt and pepper. The top should be covered with slices of potatoes. Melt the clarified butter in a small pan and pour over the ingredients. Bring the Pichelsteiner to the boil, cover and leave to simmer for 1 1/2 hours. Serve very hot with chopped parsley and chives.

Simple dishes to beer and wine

Obatzda

The name of this Bavarian cheese dish is almost self-explanatory. "Obaazn" means in Bavarian dialect to dress. In High German one would perhaps best translate this recipe as "dressed cheese".

1 small onion,
250 g mature Bavarian camembert (or other),
1 tbsp soft butter, 1 tbsp beer or sour cream,
1 tsp sweet paprika powder,
1 tsp caraway seeds,
freshly ground black pepper, salt,
2 tbsp chopped chives

Peel and finely chop the onion. Squash the camembert with a fork and mix with the butter, beer or sour cream. Add the onion, paprika powder, caraway and season to taste with a large pinch of pepper and a little salt (careful – the more mature the cheese the saltier it is). Serve the cream cheese on a wooden plate and sprinkle with chopped chives.

 This snack is best served with dark, farmer-style bread and radishes.

 This and other blends made from cheese or spiced curd can be found all over Germany. In the south one eats them as a snack to beer or wine. In the north and east it is typical to serve potatoes in their skins with these cheese dishes.

Meat balls

2 stale white bread rolls,
1 onion, 1 tsp butter,
500 g mixed minced meat,
1 large egg, salt,
freshly ground pepper,
1 tsp sharp mustard,
oil for frying

Soak the rolls in lukewarm water. Peel the onion, chop finely and fry in the heated butter until transparent. Squeeze the rolls firmly and break apart with a fork in a bowl. Add the onions, minced meat, egg, salt, pepper and mustard and stir to a homogenous meat dough. With damp hands form 12 balls and then press them flat. Heat up the oil in a pan and then fry the meat balls from both sides at middle temperature for roughly 10 minutes.

 Buletten or *Frikadellen* are a typical snack in Berlin pubs – eaten cold with a bread roll and mustard. They taste best with beer and clear, cold corn schnapps.

 The German beef steak, only made from minced beef, bread rolls, onions and spices and formerly served with fried potatoes and Teltow turnips is known today as the fast-food hamburger.

Handkäs "with music"

4 pieces of Handkäs cheese (125 g each),
2 tsp caraway seeds, freshly ground black pepper,
1/8 l apple juice, 1/8 l dry white wine,
2 tbsp fruit schnapps, 1 large red onion,
2 tbsp apple vinegar, 4 tbsp oil, salt,
1/2 bunch of parsley

2–3 days before serving cut the cheese into segments
and place in layers like roof tiles in a flat porcelain or
ceramic dish. Add caraway seeds and coarsely ground
pepper to each layer. In another bowl mix the apple
juice, wine and schnapps and then pour over the
cheese. Marinate for 2–3 days in the refrigerator and
baste regularly with the marinade.
On the day of serving peel and finely chop the onion.
Pour off the cheese marinade and mix vigorously with
oil and vinegar. Add the onion, salt and pepper and
leave to stand covered for 30 minutes.
In the meantime wash the parsley and finely chop the
leaves. Place portions of cheese on individual plates,
salt and pepper and sprinkle with parsley. Serve the
onion marinade separately with a spoon next to the
Handkäs.

 This snack is typical for many wine-growing areas.
In the Palatinate this cheese is marinated in wine.
After a few days it is ready for the "music" – the
onions. Serve with rustic rye bread and cider or
white wine.

Meat sausage salad

200 g meat sausage, 1 onion,
salt, freshly ground black pepper,
2 pickled gherkins, 6 tbsp mild vinegar,
2 tbsp gherkin juice, 3 tbsp neutral oil,
1–2 tbsp chopped chives

Skin and thinly slice the sausage. Decorate the slices in a circle on a flat dish. Peel and thinly slice the onion and cover the sausage slices. Season to taste with a little salt and ample pepper. Cut the gherkins into thin slices and spread over the salad. Mix the vinegar, gherkin juice and oil in a bowl and gently pour over the salad. Cover and marinate for 45 minutes in a cool place but not in the refrigerator.

 This snack is best served with radishes, caraway or wholemeal rolls, farmer's bread and butter.

 Also now typical for the German cuisine is the Swiss version of the Meat sausage salad which apart from sausage also includes diced Emmentaler cheese.

Schweinswürstel with sauerkraut

One can eat *Schweinswürstel* – small spicy pork sausages – all over Bavaria: at the *Oktoberfest*, at funfairs, Christmas markets and takeaways. In pubs they are usually offered as a snack between 2 pm and 6 pm when the normal kitchen is closed.

For the sauerkraut:
750 g raw sauerkraut, 1 tbsp pork dripping,
1/4 l apple juice, 1/8 l meat stock, 1 bay leaf,
3 cloves, 1 juniper berry, 3 white peppercorns
For the sausages: 2 tbsp oil, 16 pork chipolata
(small thin, sometimes spiced sausages)
or 8 large pork sausages

Squeeze out the sauerkraut and break apart with a fork. Fry in the hot dripping for about 2 minutes until brown. Pour over the apple juice and stock and bring to the boil. Add the spices, cover the saucepan and leave to simmer at medium heat for approx. 1 1/2 hours. The sauerkraut should then be soft and well cooked. For the sausages heat the oil in a large pan. Fry the sausages at low heat for 10 minutes, turning them regularly. Now the sausages have lost most of their fat. Then brown-fry the sausages for a further 5 minutes. Serve with the sauerkraut on pre-warmed plates together with rye bread rolls and semi-sharp mustard.

The sauerkraut tastes even better if it is cooked earlier and warmed up again.

Onion cake

This is a snack, served in the autumn with young wine. It is typical for southern Germany, the Palatinate and Thuringia.

For the dough: 21 g fresh yeast,
200 ml lukewarm milk, 1/2 tsp sugar,
300 g flour, 1/2 tbsp salt,
1 tsp untreated lemon peel, 2 tbsp oil
For the topping: 1 piece of streaky smoked
bacon (200 g), 2 kg onions, 1 tbsp dried marjoram,
4 tbsp oil, 500 g sour cream, 2 eggs, 1–2 tsp caraway
seeds, salt, 1/2 tsp spicy paprika powder
In addition: fat for the baking tray

For the dough mix the crumbled yeast with half the milk, the sugar and 3 tbsp of flour in a small dish and leave for 15 minutes. Mix the remaining flour and milk with salt and lemon peel in a separate bowl. Add the yeast dough mixture and oil. Stir for 10 minutes with a hand mixer using the dough hook. After this the dough should peel away from the rim of the bowl. Cover and leave to rise in a warm place for approx. 1 hour, by then the dough should have doubled in volume.
In the meantime finely dice the bacon for the topping. Peel the onions and slice in thin rings. Fry the bacon and marjoram in hot oil until crispy. Add onions and fry at low heat until tender. Remove and cool luke-warm. Mix with sour cream, eggs, caraway, salt and paprika powder.

Heat the oven 200 °C, (fan-assisted oven 180 °C, gas 3). Spread the dough evenly over a fatted baking tray and cover flatly with the filling. Cover and leave for a further 15 minutes. Place the cake on the middle rail in the pre-heated oven and bake golden-yellow for 40 minutes. Serve warm or lukewarm.

Heringshäckerle – Hashed herrings

This Silesian speciality was originally made only from salted herring, smoked bacon, onions and apples. The following recipe is now a typical Berlin dish.

2 hard-boiled eggs, 2 small onions,
1 large pickled gherkin, 1 sourish apple,
1 thin slice streaky smoked bacon,
4 herring filets, 100 g sour cream,
1 tbsp chopped parsley, salt,
freshly ground black pepper

Shell the eggs and peel the onions, dry the gherkin. Cut the apple in four, remove and discard the core. Finely chop everything. Cut the bacon and herrings into thin strips. Put all ingredients together in a bowl, add sour cream and parsley, pepper and salt and mix with a fork. Cover and put in the refrigerator for 30 minutes. Serve with dark bread and butter or potatoes in their skins.

Fish dishes

Trout "Müllerin"

4 ready prepared trout
(each approx. 350 g),
salt, freshly ground white pepper,
1 small onion, 1 tbsp chopped parsley,
2 tbsp lemon juice, 4 tbsp flour, 2 tbsp oil,
2 heaped tbsp clarified butter, 1 lemon,
8 small twigs of parsley

Wash and clean the trout thoroughly with cold water and dry. Salt and pepper the trout inside and out. Peel the onion and finely grate. Mix with the chopped parsley and lemon juice, fill the fish with the mixture. Turn the trout in the flour and remove any excess flour.
Mix the oil and clarified butter and heat up in two pans big enough for two trouts each. Fry the fish in the hot oil for 5 minutes each side. Remove and serve on pre-warmed plates. Decorate with lemon quarters and parsley twigs.

 Green and potato salads are the ideal side dishes.

 It is best to ensure that the fish have been scaled before use. This is important when frying, as the crispy outer skin can then be enjoyed as well as the fish itself.

 During frying regularly baste the fish with the hot oil. To turn the fish in the pan use a flat kitchen spatula to avoid the fish from breaking apart.

Blue trout

2 small sachets of fish herbs, 1 tbsp salt,
1/4 l apple or herb vinegar,
2 slices of lemon,
4 ready prepared trout
(each approx. 350 g)

Bring 3 l of water with the herbs, salt, vinegar and lemon slices to the boil in a large pan. Leave covered to simmer for about 15 minutes.
In the meantime cold rinse the trouts thoroughly. Then place the fish in the stock and bring the water to bubble. Reduce the heat and leave to simmer in a half closed pan for about 15 minutes. Remove the trout from the stock and serve on pre-warmed plates.

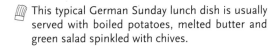 This typical German Sunday lunch dish is usually served with boiled potatoes, melted butter and green salad spinkled with chives.

Fresh trout tend to break apart when removed from the stock. So please handle them careful.

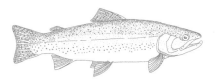

Kipper pancakes

150 g flour, 1 tsp salt, 4 eggs, 1/4 l milk,
4 kippers, clarified butter or oil for frying,
1 bundle of chives

Mix the flour with salt and the eggs. Stir in the milk and
then leave the batter to stand for 30 minutes at room
temperature.
Wash the kippers with cold water, dry and skin. Take
out the filets and cut into bite-size pieces.
Warm up the fat in a large non-stick frying pan. Pour in
a quarter of the batter and spread evenly. Cover with a
suitable number of fish pieces. Bake at low heat for
4 minutes on both sides. Keep warm in a pre-heated
oven at 50 °C until all pancakes have been cooked.
Serve with chopped chives.

 In Schleswig-Holstein green salad with a cream
dressing is served as a side dish.

Pickled fried herrings

4 ready prepared fresh herrings
(each approx. 200 g),
2 tbsp lemon juice, 2 carrots, 3 onions,
1/4 l mild vinegar, 1/8 l dry white wine,
salt, 1 tbsp sugar, 2 small sachets of dried fish herbs,
freshly ground black pepper, 50 g flour, 6 tbsp oil

A day before serving wash the herrings thoroughly in cold water and then dry them with kitchen paper. Pour over the lemon juice and leave for 10 minutes.
For the stock peel carrots and onions and slice thinly. Boil both these ingredients in 1 l of water together with the vinegar, wine, 1 tbsp of salt, sugar and fish herbs for 5 minutes. Turn off the heat and leave the stock on the hot plate. Salt and pepper the herrings inside and out and flour them all over. Fry 2 herrings at a time in hot oil for 5 minutes, basting regularly with the oil. Remove and lay the fish next to each other in a dish. When all herrings have been fried pour over the hot stock and leave uncovered to cool. Then place in the refrigerator for at least 24 hours.

 The herrings, eaten with rye bread and butter or potatoes in their skins, make up a substantial but refined meal and are a typical dish throughout Germany.

 It is very important to use mild vinegar, otherwise the herrings will become too sour.

Young herrings "housewife style"

Young herrings called "Matjes" are particularly tender, fatty and very tasty. They are conserved with salt in the same way as "normal" herrings. At times when fish was not regularly available in inland regions the herring was the most important fish – cheap, easy to get and curable; many older people can still remember the communal herring barrels which provided for several families.

8 young herring filets,
1/2 l sparkling water, 2 onions,
2 sourish apples, 150 g sour cream,
100 ml cream, 1 tsp sugar,
freshly ground white pepper,
approx. 1 tsp lemon juice,
1 tbsp chopped chives

Rinse the filets and lay in the sparkling water for 2 hours. Dry with kitchen paper and lay in a flat dish. Peel the onions and slice into thin rings. Quarter the apples, remove and discard the cores, thinly slice the quarters. Spread the two ingredients over the fish filets. Mix the cream and sour cream and season to taste with sugar, pepper and lemon juice. Pour evenly over the fish and leave covered for at least 2 hours in a cool room. When serving sprinkle with chopped chives.

Matjes taste best with potatoes in their skins or wholemeal bread and butter.

Meat dishes

Calf's liver "Berlin"

3 onions,
3 sourish apples
(Coxe Orange or Boskop),
2 tbsp lemon juice, 50 g butter,
salt, freshly ground pepper,
2 tbsp oil, 4 slices calf's liver
(each approx. 120 g)

Peel the onions, cut in half and thinly slice. Remove the apple cores using an apple corer. Peel the apples and cut into fingerbreadth slices and sprinkle with lemon juice.

Heat the butter in a large pan. Fry the apple slices for approx. 4 minutes on both sides. They should by then be soft. Keep warm on a serving plate. Fry the onions in the remaining fat until transparent and soft. Season to taste with salt and pepper and hold warm with the apples. Rinse the liver slices and dry. Add the oil to the frying fat and heat up. Fry the liver at moderately high heat for approx. 2 minutes each side. The slices should then be slightly brown and just done – one can test this by prodding a knife into the slices: if there is no blood loss they are ready. Salt and pepper the liver, serve immediately together with the apples and onions. As a side dish – mashed potatoes.

 It is important to fry the apples, onions and liver separately. In order to serve this dish really hot pre-warm the serving platter in the oven at 50 °C.

Beef roulades

2 large pickled gherkins,
1 small onion,
4 thin slices of beef
(approx. 180 g each),
salt, freshly ground black pepper,
4 tbsp hot mustard,
4 thin slices cooked ham,
1 tbsp flour, 2 tbsp clarified butter or oil,
1 tsp tomato puree, 1/4 l meat stock,
2 tbsp sour cream,
1 tbsp chopped chives

Slice the gherkins lengthwise in strips. Peel the onions and chop finely. Rinse the slices of meat, dry with kitchen paper and press flat with the ball of the hands.

Salt and pepper, spread with mustard and cover with the ham. Cover it with gherkins and onions. Roll up the meat slices and fix with a small metal skewer or kitchen thread. Turn the roulades in flour and fry at moderately high to high heat until they are brown on all sides. Add the tomato puree and approx. a third of the stock and stir to a gravy. Slowly pour in the rest of the stock and let it slowly thicken. Cook the roulades gently, covered, for 1 1/2 hours. Remove the roulades and keep warm on pre-warmed plates. Stir the sour cream into the gravy and taste again. Pour over the roulades and sprinkle with chives.

Germans usually enjoy this popular meal with Brussel sprouts or red cabbage, boiled potatoes or ribbon noodles.

Rheinisch sour roast

For 6 portions
1 kg beef, 1/4 l white wine vinegar,
a piece of cinnamon stick,
5 juniper berries,
10 black peppercorns, 1 bay leaf,
1 twig of fresh thyme,
salt, freshly ground white pepper,
1 small carrot, 100 g celeriac,
1 small leek, 1 onion, 2 tbsp oil,
1 slice of dark rye bread,
100 g raisins, 2 tbsp sour cream,
1 tbsp raspberry or
white balsamic vinegar

3 days in advance place the rinsed piece of beef in a glass or porcelain bowl. Boil up 3/8 l of water together with the vinegar, cinnamon stick, juniper berries, peppercorns, bay leaf and thyme. Let cool and then pour over the meat. Cover and keep for 3 days in the refrigerator, turning at regular intervals.

To prepare the meat for cooking remove from the vinegar marinade and dry. Rub salt and pepper all over the meat. Pour the marinade through a colander. Approx. 3/8 l should be kept for cooking. Peel or prepare the vegetables and dice finely.

Warm up the oil in a roasting tin. Sear the roast at high heat until brown all over. Remove and place on a plate. Sear the diced vegetables and onion in the remaining fat. Pour the 3/8 l marinade and stir until it thickens. Crumble the bread, add to the gravy and stir until it has dissolved. Replace the meat into the baking tin, replace lid and cook gently for 2 1/2 hours until tender. Baste regularly and if necessary add marinade. Remove the meat, cover with tin foil and leave to rest. Keep warm. Sieve the gravy into a saucepan. Press out all the remains of the ingredients and dispose. Stir the raisins and sour cream into the gravy and bring shortly to the boil. Add salt, pepper and vinegar and season to taste. Slice the roast meat and arrange on pre-warmed plates. Pour gravy over the meat and serve with salad and potato dumplings.

 The rye bread thickens the sauce and provides a slightly sour taste.

 In Bavaria and the Palatinate a special gingerbread for sauces is used instead of rye bread and no raisins.

Roast pork

For 6 Portions
1,5 kg pork with fat and outer rind
(e.g. shoulder, please note the first tip),
salt, freshly ground black pepper,
1 tsp caraway seeds,
1 large onion, 1 large carrot,
1 piece of stale rye bread crust,
approx. 1/2 l dark beer

Pre-heat the oven to 220 °C (fan-assisted oven 200 °C, gas 5). Rinse the meat and dry. Rub in salt and pepper over the whole joint, place rind down into a baking tin and sprinkle with caraway seeds. Peel the onion and carrot, dice finely and spread together with the bread around the meat. Pour over 1/4 l of hot water. Cook the meat, uncovered, in the pre-warmed oven for 20 minutes on the lowest rail. By this time the water should have evaporated. Turn the joint over and pour over half of the beer. Turn down the oven temperature to 180 °C (fan-assisted oven 160 °C, gas 2) and cook the meat for a further 1 1/2 hours. In this time regularly baste the meat adding the remaining beer. Turn the oven up to 220 °C (fan-assisted oven 200 °C, gas 5) and roast the meat for another 30 minutes until the rind becomes crispy. Take the meat out of the baking tin and put it back into oven on a platter. Leave the oven door open. Pour the roasting fat through a colander into a saucepan, press out the vegetables and bread and dispose. Bring the gravy to the boil and season to taste with salt and pepper. Slice the pork and put on individual plates. Pour a little gravy over the meat and serve the rest separately.

 The requested piece of meat is part of the shoulder which still has the rind. It is recommended to ask the butcher to make diamond cuts in the skin as this task requires a very sharp knife and a lot of practice.

 In Bavaria the roast is served with cucumber salad and the Bavarians pour gravy over the salad to make it really slushy. An authentic side dish is of course bread dumplings (ref: recipe for creamy mushrooms and bread dumplings, p. 64) or potato dumplings. Most people prefer to buy quality ready prepared dough in the supermarket.

 Do not cover the roast with tin foil while keeping it warm in the oven otherwise the outer skin will become soggy.

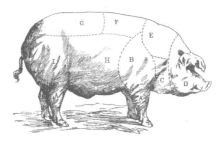

Creamy goulash

This Bavarian speciality is known regionally as "einge-machtes Kalbfleisch". The word "einmach" refers to the white creamy sauce served to the veal.

600 g boneless veal (ask your butcher
for advice), 2 onions, 1 tbsp oil,
1 tbsp clarified butter,
1 tbsp tomato purée, 1 tsp flour,
1 tsp sweet paprika powder,
approx. 1/4 l meat stock, salt,
1 piece of untreated lemon peel,
cayenne pepper, 120 g sour cream,
1–2 tbsp chopped parsley

Rinse and dry the meat and cut up into 2 cm large chunks. Peel the onions and chop finely.
Heat the fat in a baking tin. Sharp-fry the meat until brown all over. Reduce the heat, add the onions and fry until transparent. Then add the tomato purée, flour and paprika and stir the ingredients for a few seconds. Pour in the stock. Add salt and lemon peel. Bring the goulash to the boil and then simmer for 1 hour until tender. If necessary add more stock. Add the sour cream, increase the heat but do not boil. Season to taste and serve sprinkled with parsley.

 This dish is best served with bread dumplings (ref: recipe for creamy mushrooms and bread dumplings, p. 64), ribbon noodles or *Spätzle* (ref:

recipe for *Allgäuer Kässpatzn*, p. 59). The *Spätzle* for the goulash should be prepared with water instead of milk and without cheese and onions.

Tellerfleisch – Boiled meat in broth

1 onion, 1 small carrot, 100 g celeriac,
1 small leek, 1 bay leaf, 4 soup bones,
600 g of boiling beef (eg. lean ox breast,
ask your butcher for advice),
salt, 1 horseradish (approx. 20 cm),
4 large pickled gherkins, 2 bundles of chives

Peel and halve the onion. Peal or prepare and dice carrot, celeriac and leek. Bring to the boil in 3 l of water together with the bay leaf and the cleaned bones. Simmer gently covered for 1 hour. Rinse and add the piece of meat, add salt and bring gently to the boil. Then simmer for 1 1/2–2 hours until tender.
In the meantime peel the horseradish, rinse and grate. Thinly slice the gherkins. Remove the meat from the stock, slice and put into soup plates. Pour over some stock and sprinkle with horseradish and chives. Serve the gherkins separately.

 Throughout Germany this dish is usually eaten with boiled potatoes and savoy cabbage or potato salad. In Bavaria this dish is also served with pretzels and mild mustard. In Hessen and Berlin with potatoes boiled in the broth.

Königsberger Klopse
– Königsberg meat dumplings

This dish of meat dumplings is served in a white sauce, spiced with anchovies, capers and lemon. It originates from the former province of East Prussia but is now a classic dish throughout Germany.

2 slightly stale wheat bread rolls,
1 onion, 2 anchovy filets,
1 small untreated lemon,
500 g mixed minced meat,
1 egg, 2 tbsp breadcrumbs,
3 tbsp chopped parsley, salt,
fresh black pepper,
3/4 l meat stock,
1/8 l dry white wine,
1 bay leaf, 4 white peppercorns,
50 g butter, 40 g flour, 125 g sour cream,
1 egg yolk, 2–3 tbsp capers,
a little sugar, freshly grated nutmeg,
a little lemon juice according to taste

Soak the bread rolls in lukewarm water. Press out excess water. Peel the onions and dice finely. Cold rinse the anchovy filets, dry and cut finely. Wash and halve the lemon. Thinly cut a large piece of the peel of one half and chop finely. Squeeze out the juice. Peel the other half, cut into small pieces and put aside.

Mix together the minced meat with the bread rolls onion, anchovies, lemon peel, 1 tbsp lemon juice, egg, breadcrumbs and half of the parsley until the mixture is firm. With damp hands form 16 dumplings. Bring the stock with the wine, bay leaf, peppercorns and the remaining lemon juice to the boil in a saucepan. Add the dumplings and simmer half covered for 10 minutes. Then take the dumplings out and place in a pre-warmed dish. Add 2 tbsp of stock, cover and keep warm.

Heat the butter in a saucepan until bubbles appear. Add the flour and stir until golden yellow. Pour the stock slowly through a sieve and stir until the sauce is smooth. Lightly boil covered for 10 minutes.

Whip the sour cream and egg yolk, mix in several spoonfulls of the sauce and add the mixture to the sauce, heat up again but no longer boil. Add the capers, lemon pieces, and the remaining parsley. Season to taste with sugar, nutmeg, salt, pepper and lemon juice. Add the dumplings to the sauce and leave to draw in the covered pan for 5 minutes.

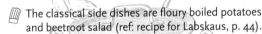 The classical side dishes are floury boiled potatoes and beetroot salad (ref: recipe for Labskaus, p. 44).

Knuckle of pork with mashed peas

200 g dried yellow split peas,
approx. 2 kg salted or cured leg
or knuckle of pork
(ask your butcher for advice),
2 large onions, 2 cloves,
1 small carrot, 100 g celeriac,
1 small leek, a little piece of cinnamon stick,
3 juniper berries, 5 black peppercorns,
1 bay leaf, 1 twig of fresh thyme,
1 piece of streaky smoked bacon (100 g),
1 tbsp clarified butter or oil,
salt and freshly ground pepper

On the day previous to cooking soak the peas in cold water for approx. 12 hours. On the next day rinse the knuckle of pork with cold water, bring to the boil in a saucepan in 3 l of water and then leave to simmer gently for 1 hour. Scoop off the foam in the water regularly. Peel 1 onion, stick with the cloves and place in the water with the meat. Peal or prepare carrot, celeriac and leek. Add the vegetables whole together with cinnamon, juniper, peppercorns, bay leaf and rinsed thyme. Leave the meat to simmer for a further 1 1/2 hours until tender.

At the same time sieve and rinse the peas with cold water. Boil the peas in 1/2 l of water and then simmer for approx. 1 1/2 hours until soft. If the peas are too dry add a little meat stock. Peel the second onion and thinly slice. Remove the rind and gristle from the bacon and dice. Heat up the fat in a pan. Gently fry the bacon, add the onions and fry golden yellow.

Mash the peas with a hand mixer adding hot stock until the mashed peas have the consistency of mashed potatoes. Season to taste with salt and pepper. Place the knuckle of pork on a pre-warmed platter. Put the peas in a bowl and top with the bacon and onions. Serve piping hot together with sauerkraut (ref: recipe for Schweinswürstel with sauerkraut, p. 21) and with mashed potatoes.

 This recipe is typical for Berlin. In the south of Germany the knuckle is cooked like beef in stock and is served with root vegetables and freshly grated horseradish. In the west of Germany sauerkraut is served as a side dish together with mashed potatoes.

Labskaus

1 kg salted beef
(e.g. breast, ask your butcher for advice),
3 onions, 2 cloves, 2 bay leaves,
1 tsp white peppercorns,
750 g waxy potatoes,
2 tbsp pork dripping,
salt, freshly ground pepper,
Worcester sauce,
5 large pickled gherkins,
4 eggs, 1 tbsp butter,
4 young herring filets (Matjes)

Cut the meat into large chunks, peel 1 onion and stick with the cloves. Put the meat, onion, bay leaves and peppercorns into a saucepan. Pour over 1 1/2 l of boiling water, bring to the boil and leave to simmer, covered, for 1 1/2 hours. In the meantime peel and dice the potatoes and boil until really soft.

Pour of the water and add a little meat stock to the potatoes. Mash thoroughly. Take the meat out of the stock and mince it in a mincing machine.

Peel the remaining onions, dice finely and fry gently in the dripping until they become transparent. Stir in the minced meat, adding meat stock until the mixture has the consistency of thick cream. Add the mashed potatoes and stock until the mixture begins to thicken. Season to taste with a little salt, a good pinch of pepper and several dashes of Worcester sauce and leave covered for 20 minutes to simmer gently. Finely dice the gherkins and mix into the Labskaus. Fry the eggs in butter. Serve the Labskaus on individual plates topped with the egg and decorate with the young herrings.

A typical side dish to Labskaus is beetroot salad: for this boil 750 g beetroots in plenty of water for 35–40 minutes until just tender. Rinse under cold water, peel and slice thinly. Mix with a mixture of 6 tbsp red wine vinegar, 1 tbsp hot mustard and 3 tbsp oil. Season to taste with salt and freshly ground pepper.

Chicken ragout

1 large carrot, 200 g celeriac,
1 large leek, 1 onion, 1 bunch of parsley,
1 twig of fresh thyme,
4 white peppercorns, 1 bay leaf,
500 g chicken breast,
1 heaped tsp salt, 1 tsp chicken stock extract,
60 g butter, 50 g flour, 150 g deep frozen peas,
150 g tinned sliced mushrooms,
1 large piece of untreated lemon peel,
3–4 tbsp lemon juice, 100 ml cream,
1 egg yolk, freshly ground white pepper

Peal or prepare carrot, celeriac and leek and cut into small pieces. Peel and halve the onion. Rinse the parsley and thyme. Boil up all these ingredients together with the peppercorns and bay leaf in 1 l of water and leave to simmer gently for 15 minutes. Rinse the chicken and put in the water together with salt and the stock extract and simmer gently for 15 minutes until the meat is tender. Remove the meat and cut up into small chunks. Pour the stock through a sieve. Dispose of the vegetables and spices.

Heat up the butter in a saucepan until it begins to froth, mix in the flour and heat up until golden yellow. Slowly pour in the stock and stir until the sauce has a smooth consistency. Add the frozen peas, drained mushrooms and the lemon peel. Bring the sauce to the boil and leave to simmer gently for 10 minutes. Add the meat and 2 tbsp of lemon juice and stir well. Whisk the cream with the egg yolk and mix with several spoonfuls of the hot sauce. Then pour into the sauce and heat up everything once again but do not boil. Season the ragout with salt, pepper and lemon juice to taste and serve with boiled rice.

 At one time chicken ragout was a festive meal which was served in a ring of rice. For this you need 500 g cooked long-grain rice. Butter a circle mould. Add 1 tbsp of butter to the rice and mix with a fork. Spread the rice evenly into the mould and turn upside down onto a pre-warmed platter. Decorate the ragout in the middle of the rice ring and serve immediately.

 An innovative variation makes use of fresh white asparagus instead of the frozen peas together with fresh mushrooms. A handful of capers gives this dish a particular tasty touch.

Game goulash with cranberry sauce

750 g boneless game goulash in chunks,
50 g streaky smoked bacon,
1 small carrot, 100 g celeriac,
1 small leek, 1 small onion, 2 tbsp oil,
1 tbsp flour, 200 ml game stock (glass),
1/4 l dry red wine, salt,
freshly ground white pepper,
400 g fresh cranberries,
1/4 tsp gingerbread spice,
1 piece of untreated orange peel,
1 tbsp redcurrant jelly, 2 tbsp brandy

Rinse and dry the meat. Cut off all tendons. Finely dice the bacon. Peal or prepare carrot, celeriac, leek and onion and finely dice.

Heat the oil in a stewing pot. Sharp-fry the meat until brown all over. Add the bacon, vegetables and onion. Sprinkle everything with flour and continue to stir fry for 1–2 minutes. Slowly pour in the game stock, mix well until the sauce begins to thicken. Add approx. half of the red wine and bring to the boil. Salt and pepper the goulash meat and leave covered to simmer gently for 1 1/2 hours.

In the meantime wash and dry the cranberries. In a saucepan boil up the cranberries with the rest of the red wine, add the gingerbread spice and orange peel and leave to simmer for 5 minutes. Add to the goulash and leave to simmer for a further 15 minutes. Flavour to taste with redcurrant jelly, brandy, salt and pepper.

 This autumnal, tasty goulash is best served with ribbon noodles or *Spätzle* (ref: recipe for *Allgäuer Kässpatzn*, p. 59). The *Spätzle* for the game goulash should be prepared with water instead of milk and without cheese and onions. Serve immediately with butter in pre-warmed bowls. If fresh cranberries are not available these can be replaced with dried or deep frozen berries.

Vegetable, potatoe and noodle dishes

Farmer's breakfast

500 g cooked cold potatoes in the skin,
1 onion, 100 g boiled ham,
2 tbsp clarified butter or oil,
salt, freshly ground white pepper,
4 eggs, 2 tbsp cream,
1 tbsp chopped chives,
2–3 large pickled gherkins

Slice the peeled potatoes and cut the peeled onion into fine rings. Cut the ham in strips.
Heat up 1 tbsp of the fat in a large non-stick frying pan. Fry half the potatoes over moderately high heat from all sides. Add half of the onions and ham and gently fry until transparent. Salt and pepper. Stir two eggs and 1 tbsp of cream and pour over the potatoes. Leave until lightly set. Halve and place on two pre-warmed plates and serve with chives and gherkins cut fan shape. Cook the second portion with the remaining ingredients as above.

Cabbage roulades

This is a traditional winter dish: white, red and savoy cabbage belong to the vegetables which were stored after the autumn harvest and were available until spring. For hundreds of years housewives used cabbage together with left-over meat, bread and/or potatoes to make a tasty dish which is still enjoyed today. Cabbage roulades were always eaten throughout Germany when one could not afford to cook meat roulades. In earlier days housewives who didn't have to turn every penny around made out of thrift a virtue – it was quite normal to use up leftovers.

1 white cabbage (1 kg),
For the filling: 1 large onion,
1 slightly stale wheat bread roll,
5 tbsp hot milk, 1 bunch of parsley,
250 g mixed minced meat,
2 tbsp chopped parsley,
1 small egg, 1 tbsp capers, salt
In addition: 2 tbsp oil or clarified butter,
1/8 l meat or vegetable stock,
100 g cream, 1 tbsp chopped chives

For the filling: sprinkle the milk over the finely diced bread roll and allow to soak. Peel and finely chop the onion. Rinse and dry the parsley, remove from the stalks and finely chop the leaves. Mix the bread, onion, parsley, minced meat, egg, capers and a good pinch of salt. Bring ample water to the boil in a large saucepan.

Remove the outer leaves of the cabbage. Place the whole cabbage in the water and boil for about 10 minutes. By then the cabbage leaves should be easy to peel off. Take the cabbage out of the water and leave to cool slightly. Remove the leaves from the stalk with a small knife. Take 8 large leaves and cut the thick ribs flat. Cut the rest of the cabbage into strips. Lay the 4 largest leaves next to each other on a working surface, place the 4 smaller ones on top.

Spread the meat mixture evenly on the leaves, fold in the sides of the leaves, roll up and tie together with kitchen thread.

Heat the fat in a casserole. Briskly fry the roulades from all sides. Add the stock, boil up and leave the roulades to simmer in the covered casserole for 20 minutes. Arrange the cabbage strips around the roulades and pour over the cream. Return to the boil and leave to simmer for a further 10–15 minutes. Serve the roulades and cabbages strips on pre-warmed plates and sprinkle with chives. As a side dish: boiled potatoes.

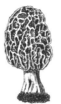

Leipziger Allerlei
– Mixed spring vegetables

200 g fine green beans, 100 g snow peas,
1 small cauliflower, 200 g white asparagus,
1 small cabbage turnip, 2 carrots,
200 g fresh morels, salt,
1 tbsp sugar, 100 g butter,
100 g shrimp or crab butter (glass),
freshly ground pepper,
2 tbsp chopped parsley

Prepare and wash the beans and snow peas. Cut the cauliflower into florets core and discard the stem.
Peel the stalks of the asparagus and trim the bases. Remove the tips and put aside. Cut the stalks into finger-width pieces. Peel the cabbage turnip and carrots and cut into pencil-thick and 5–6 cm long pieces. Thoroughly wash the morels.
Pre-warm a large serving platter at 50 °C. Bring ample water to the boil a large saucepan. Add 1 tbsp of salt, sugar and 1 tbsp of butter. Add the beans, cauliflower, pieces of asparagus, cabbage turnip and carrots and

allow to boil gently for 10 minutes. Remove the vegetables with a skimmer and sway dry in a large colander. Gently warm up the shrimp or crab butter in a large pot. Add the vegetables, season with pepper and turn over in the butter. Spread on the serving platter, keep warm in the oven. Place the snow peas and asparagus tips in the still boiling water and gently boil for 5 minutes. Remove, sway dry and turn over in the remaining shrimp butter. Season with pepper and add to the other vegetables.

Gently melt the remaining butter in a large pan. Increase the heat and briskly fry the morels for 2 minutes, turning constantly. Cover and leave for 3 minutes at medium heat. Salt and pepper and add to the other vegetables. Pour over the remaining butter and shrimp or crab butter and sprinkle with parsley. Serve immediately.

 The *Leipziger Allerlei* is the finest form of middle-class spring cuisine with it's firm vegetables and fresh morels. In earlier days this dish was prepared even more extravagantly: the whole boiled cauliflower was the centrepiece on the platter. The rest of the vegetables were cooked in béchamel sauce arranged around the cauliflower, garnished with crayfish meat. It was served with walnut-sized bread dumplings (ref: recipe for creamy mushrooms and bread dumplings, p. 64).

 Not traditional but excellent: new potatoes and stir-fried shrimps as side dishes.

Himmel und Erde – Heaven and earth

People in the Rhineland are great potato eaters – they love to eat their precious apples (groving in the heaven, German: Himmel) and potatoes (growing in the earth, German: Erde) with fried black pudding.

For the potatoes: 1 kg floury potatoes, salt,
1/8 l vegetable stock, 70 g butter, 200 ml milk
For the apple sauce: 1 kg apples (Coxe orange or
Boscop), 2 tbsp apple juice, 1 tbsp sugar,
2 tbsp lemon juice
In addition: freshly ground pepper, freshly grated
nutmeg, 4 onions, 4 slices black pudding (50 g each)

Peel and dice the potatoes. Gently boil up them in the salted stock for about 15 minutes until done. Coarsely mash the potatoes in the stock, mixing with 50 g butter and the milk.

In the meantime peel and quarter the apples. Remove and discard the cores and cut the quarters in thin wedges. Boil up with the apple juice, sugar and lemon juice and leave to steam gently for about 10 minutes. Mix the apple sauce into the potatoes, season to taste with salt, pepper and nutmeg and keep warm in a pre-warmed oven at 50 °C. Peel the onions and cut into thin rings. Fry in a non-stick pan in the remaining butter until transparent. Arrange on top of the mashed potatoes and apples. Fry the black pudding slices on each side for 1 minute in the remaining fat. Add on top of the onions and serve immediately.

Potato pancakes with apple sauce

1 kg moderately waxy potatoes,
1 egg, 1 tbsp breadcrumbs, salt,
freshly ground pepper,
oil for frying, 1 recipe for apple sauce
(ref: recipe for Himmel und Erde p. 56)

Peel and wash the potatoes. Grate but not too fine.
Mix together with the egg and breadcrumbs, pepper
and salt.
Heat up plenty of oil in a large non-stick frying pan. For
each pancake take 2 tbsp of dough, place in the pan
and press flat. Fry the pancakes over moderately high
heat on both sides for 5 minutes. Remove and dry on
kitchen paper and keep warm in a pre-heated oven at
50 °C until all pancakes have been fried. Serve with the
apple sauce.

 In the Rhineland the pancakes are eaten as fol-
lows: Place a pancake on a thin slice of pumper-
nickel and eat it with the cold apple sauce. Coffee
with milk and sugar is drunk to this dish. In nor-
thern Germany the pancakes are always served
with apple sauce, in Bavaria with sauerkraut.

Potatoes in their jackets
with green sauce

This dish is typical for Frankfurt where the green sauce is also eaten with moderately soft boiled eggs or boiled beef. The herbs required in Germany can be found at most markets or greengrocers. Please ask your greengrocer for the mixture.

1,5 kg small new potatoes,
2 bunches of mixed herbs (parsley, chives,
chervil, watercress, borage, sorrel and dill),
2 tsp lemon juice, 4 hard boiled eggs,
250 g sour cream, 150 g low-fat yogurt,
1 tbsp hot mustard, 3 tbsp oil,
salt, freshly ground white pepper

Wash the potatoes und soft boil in a little water. Rinse, dry and finely chop the herbs removing the hard stalks. Mix the herbs with the lemon juice and leave covered, to stand for 15 minutes.
In the meantime shell the eggs and finely chop. Mix with the sour cream, yogurt and mustard, adding oil at intervals. Mix in the herbs. Season to taste with pepper and salt. Pour off the potatoes and leave to steam off. Peel and serve hot with the sauce.

Allgäuer Kässpatzn
– Allgäu cheese noodles

This is one of the most famous recipes in southern Germany. Take the special grater required for *Spätzle* home from your next trip to Germany. You won't regret it!

350 g flour, 3 small eggs, salt,
1/4 l milk, 200 g Allgäu Emmental cheese
in thin slices, 300 g onions, 3 tbsp oil,
2 tbsp butter, freshly ground black pepper

Briskly mix the flour with the eggs and a pinch of salt. Add the milk and stir briskly until the dough is foamy. Leave covered to rest until the onions and cheese have been prepared. Dice the cheese (not too small pieces otherwise the *Spätzle* will become soggy). Peel the onions and grate in thin slices.
Heat up the oil and butter in a large frying pan and gently fry the onions golden brown for 20 minutes, turning regularly. At the same time boil up plenty of salted water in a large saucepan. Grate the dough portionwise through a special grater for *Spätzle* into the boiling water. Leave to boil for 1–2 minutes until the *Spätzle* float on the top of the water. Remove each portion with a skimmer, drip off well and place in a pre-warmed bowl. Sprinkle with cheese and pepper and keep warm, covered, in the oven at 50 °C. Finally add the fried onions. Serve hot with tomato or cucumber salad.

Swabian Maultaschen with spinach

For the dough:
approx. 300 g flour, 1 tsp salt, 3 large eggs
For the filling:
300 g spinach, 1 small onion,
50 g streaky smoked bacon, 2 tbsp oil,
100 g veal sausage meat or minced beef,
4 tbsp breadcrumbs, salt, freshly ground pepper,
freshly grated nutmeg, 1 dried marjoram
In addition:
extra flour for dusting, salt, 60 g butter

For the dough vigorously knead the flour, salt and eggs with the hands to make a homogenous mass. If necessary add a little more flour. Wrap the dough in cling film and leave to rest for 1 hour at room temperature. In the meantime wash, sort and prepare the spinach for the filling. Boil in sufficient water for 2 minutes. Pour through a sieve, drip off and leave to cool. Squeeze with the hands and finely chop. Finely dice the peeled onion and the bacon and gently fry in hot oil until transparent. Add, slightly cooled, to the spinach. Mix in the sausage meat or minced meat and 2 tbsp of breadcrumbs. Season to taste with salt, pepper, nutmeg and marjoram and mix well.

Divide the dough into 2 portions and roll out on flour as thinly as possible. Cut each slab into 6 by 12 cm squares and brush the edges with a little water. Spread the spinach evenly in the middle of the squares, fold together and press the edges firmly together with the prongs of a fork.

Bring adequate salted water to boil in a large saucepan. Gently simmer the *Maultaschen* in the water for just under 10 minutes.

In the meantime melt the butter in the pan. Gently fry the remaining breadcrumbs golden brown. Remove the *Maultaschen* from the water with a skimmer, drip off well, and put into pre-warmed plates. Sprinkle with the breadcrumbed butter.

 This recipe is a main meal. The Swabians also enjoy their *Maultaschen* in soup. This is how they are prepared for this: divide the dough into two or three portion and roll out each until it is as thick as the back of a knife. Leave to dry for 30 minutes. Spread the filling onto the rolled out dough leaving a finger-width at the edges. Roll the dough together. Cut off from each roll 5 cm pieces (*Maultaschen*), using the handle of a wooden cooking spoon. Gently simmer over moderately high heat in sufficient meat broth.

Ham noodles

There are only a few typical German noodle dishes as we actually prefer to eat potatoes, *Spätzle* and dumplings – Italian pasta and of course this dish.

250 g broad ribbon noodles, salt,
2 tsp butter, 200 g boiled ham, 4 eggs, 4 tbsp milk,
freshly ground black pepper, freshly grated nutmeg,
4 tbsp oil, 4 tbsp chopped parsley

Briskly boil the noodles in enough salted water, 1 minute less than suggested on the package. Pour off the water and mix with butter so that they do not stick together. While the noodles are boiling dice the ham and mix the eggs with the milk, salt, pepper and nutmeg. Heat the oil in a large non-stick frying pan. Gently fry the noodles and ham for about 1 minute, turning regularly. Pour over the eggs and leave for 3 minutes to become creamy. Fry the noodles for a further 2 minutes, turning regularly. Serve sprinkled with parsley.

White asparagus with egg sauce

An opulent traditional dish: the creamy sauce is often referred to in old cook books as "dutch sauce" (Sauce hollandaise). The egg sauce is lighter than the original but goes equally well with asparagus and tastes excellent with new potatoes.

2 kg white asparagus, 1 full tsp salt, 1/4 tsp sugar,
60 g butter, 50 g flour, 100 ml cream, 2 egg yolks,
1 tbsp chopped dill, freshly ground white pepper,
1–2 tsp lemon juice

Peel the stalks of the asparagus and trim the bases. Bring 2 l of water to the boil, add the salt and the sugar. Place the asparagus in the boiling water and cook over moderate heat for 15–20 minutes until tender but still firm to bite. Place on to a well pre-warmed platter, pour over a little of the hot asparagus stock and keep covered warm until the sauce is made. Measure 3/8 l of the stock for the sauce.
Melt the butter in a saucepan. Mix in the flour and fry golden brown. Pour in the asparagus stock slowly, boil the sauce and continue stirring until smooth. Cover the pan and leave to gently boil for about 10 minutes. Whisk the cream with the eggs. Take 3–4 tbsp from the hot sauce and stir in. Take the saucepan off the heat. Stir in the egg cream into the sauce and heat up again but do not let it boil. Mix in the dill, season to taste with salt, pepper and lemon juice and either pour over the asparagus or serve separately.

Creamy mushrooms and bread dumplings

Mushrooms in cream also known as "Schwammerl soup" was formerly the typical meal for the dairy farmers in the mountains – of course made from self picked mushrooms. The mushrooms are served in proper style in a soup plate, topped with freshly cooked, steaming dumplings and sprinkled with parsley.

For the dumplings:
10 slightly stale light wheat bread rolls
from the previous day (approx. 500 g),
salt, 1/4 l lukewarm milk, 1 onion,
50 g butter, 2 eggs, 1 tbsp chopped parsley
For the mushrooms:
1 small onion, 1 kg mixed champignons
and oyster mushrooms, 2 tbsp butter,
1 tbsp chopped parsley, 1 tbsp flour,
1/4 l cream, salt, freshly ground white pepper,
1 tbsp lemon juice
In addition:
1 tbsp parsley to decorate

For the dumplings cut the rolls in very thin slices, place in a bowl and sprinkle with 2 tsp salt. Pour over the milk. Leave covered to draw for about 20 minutes, by which time the milk should have been soaked up. Peel and finely chop the onion and fry in the heated butter, until transparent, then leave to cool. Boil up plenty of salted water in a large saucepan.

Add the onions and the frying fat, eggs and parsley to the bread, knead with the hands to make a homogenous mass. With damp hands make 12 dumplings. Place them in the hot water and quickly bring to the boil in the covered saucepan. Turn back the heat and leave to simmer half covered for about 20 minutes. In the meantime for the mushrooms peal and finely chop the onion. Clean the champignons and cut in very thin slices. Remove the stalks from the oyster mushrooms and cut the mushrooms into thin strips.

Heat the butter and gently fry the onion with the parsley until the onion is transparent. Add all mushrooms; briskly stir fry for about 2 minutes. Mix in the flour and leave covered to gently cook for 5 minutes, during which the mushrooms will loose liquid. Mix in the cream and return to the boil. Season to taste with salt, pepper and lemon juice and serve, sprinkled with parsley.

Desserts and cakes

Rote Grütze – Red fruit jelly

The authentic north German Rote Grütze is soft and is served in soup plates with ice-cold milk, cream or custard according to taste.

> 1 glass sour cherries (350 g),
> 1 packet deep frozen mixed berries (300 g),
> 1 piece untreated lemon peel,
> 2 level tbsp vanilla pudding powder,
> 1/8 l apple juice,
> 1 glass cranberry sauce (100 g),
> 2–3 tbsp sugar

Bring the cherries and juice, deep frozen berries and lemon peel shortly to the boil. Mix the apple juice and pudding powder and add to the berries. Continue to stir until firm. Mix in the cranberry sauce, season to taste with sugar. Cover and allow to cool for 2 hours.

Rice pudding with cinnamon and sugar

Originally this was a childrens' dish. But now children are fed from glasses, many adults enjoy this rice pudding as a convenience product from the supermarket. Try to cook it yourself, soft and creamy – delicious!

Approx. 400 ml milk, 1 tsp butter,
a large piece of untreated lemon peel,
100 g short-grain rice, 100 g sugar,
1 tbsp cinnamon, 100 ml cream

Bring the milk, butter and lemon peel to the boil. Stir well. Add the rice and simmer over lowest heat gently for 25 minutes. After that the rice should be soft but still grainy and fairly moist. If necessary add a little more milk when simmering. Remove the lemon peel. Whip the cream and add to the rice. Mix the cinnamon and sugar. Serve the hot pudding immediately in soup plates and sprinkle with cinnamon sugar.

Cherry casserole

In Baden and the Palatinate this dish is called "Kersch-plotzer", in Bavaria "Kirschenmichel". This dish can be served hot from the oven as a warm main meal, or eaten cold to a cup of coffee.

6 slightly stale light wheat bread,
3/8 l lukewarm milk, 750 g cherries, 4 eggs,
100 g soft butter, 75 g sugar, 1 tsp vanilla sugar,
1 pinch of salt, the grated peel of half an untreated
lemon, a little lemon juice, 50 g almond slices,
butter for the baking dish and for garnishing,
1 tbsp icing sugar

Finely dice the bread rolls, pour over the milk and leave to draw until the other ingredients have been prepared. Wash the cherries and remove the stones. Pre-heat the oven to 180 °C (fan-assisted oven 160 °C, gas 2). Separate the egg yolks from the whites. Cream the butter with sugar and vanilla sugar until light and fluffy. First add the egg yolks, salt and lemon peel and then mix in the bread rolls. Whip the egg whites and a few drops lemon juice briskly and mix into the dough. Finally mix in the cherries and almonds. Fill the dough into a fatted deep casserole, garnish with butter and sprinkle with icing sugar. Bake in a pre-warmed oven (lower tray) for approx. 1 hour. Cover with tin foil after 30 minutes to avoid the top from burning.

Apple pancakes

Germans really love pancakes. Apart from the classic apple pancake there is the north German cherry pancake with cinnamon sugar, the Bavarian plum pancake and the blueberry summer pancake – eaten throughout Germany (ref: tip). But many savoury variations made from salted batter with bacon or raw ham are very popular too – especially in Westphalia.

200 g flour, a pinch of salt, 1 tbsp vanilla sugar,
1 tsp untreated lemon peel, 4 eggs, 1/2 l milk,
4 medium size sourish and soft apples (e.g. Boskop),
4 tbsp clarified butter, cinnamon sugar to sprinkle

Mix the flour, salt, vanilla sugar, lemon peel and the eggs in a bowl. Pour in the milk and stir into a smooth batter. Leave covered to settle for 30 minutes. In the meantime quarter and peel the apples, remove and discard the cores and cut the quarters into slices.
Heat up 1 tbsp of clarified butter in a non-stick frying pan. Add a quarter of the batter. Arrange apple slices in a star shape and briskly fry the pancake for 2 minutes then turn and fry for a further 3 minutes. With remaining batter fry 3 more pancakes as above. Sprinkle with cinnamon sugar when serving.

 When making blueberry pancakes separate the egg yolks and whites. Add the stiffly whipped egg whites to the batter shortly before frying. Instead

of the apples take 600 g rinsed and dried blue-
berries. Portion these on the batter accordingly
and after approx. 5 minutes sprinkle with sugar.
Sugar again just before serving.

Mohnpielen – Poppy pudding

This is a traditional dish at Christmas and New Year in
Berlin and Brandenburg. Lots of little poppy seeds
should ensure lots of coins in the pocket.

2 sweet raisin bread rolls
from the previous day (approx. 100 g),
1/2 l milk, 100 g sugar,
possibly 2 tbsp rum, 150 g ground poppy seeds,
50 g raisins, 50 g almonds slices,
icing sugar for garnishing

Thinly slice the bread rolls and spread the slices evenly in a deep platter. Heat up the milk with the sugar and
rum. Carefully pour approx. half over the bread. Mix the
poppy seeds into the remaining boiling milk, add the
raisins and almonds. Turn off the heat and leave to
draw for 10 minutes. Layer the bread and the poppy-
seed-mixture in a glass bowl with poppies as the top
layer. Cover the bowl and leave to settle for 2 hours.
Serve sprinkled with icing sugar.

Apple cake

This cake has been popular in Germany for generations. Depending on the season one can bake it as well with stoned cherries or plums or stoned and peeled apricots.

125 g soft butter, 100 g sugar,
1 tbsp vanilla sugar, 1 pinch of salt,
1 tsp untreated lemon peel,
3 eggs, 200 g flour,
2 tsp baking powder,
fat for the baking tin,
750 g sourish and soft apples
(e.g. Boskop),
3–4 tbsp apple, quince or redcurrant jelly,
icing sugar to sprinkle

Pre-heat the oven to 180 °C (fan-assisted oven 160 °C, gas 3). Cream the butter with sugar, vanilla sugar, salt and lemon peel until light and fluffy. Add one after another the eggs, then a mixture of flour and baking powder. Spread the dough evenly in a fatted loose-bottomed cake tin (26 cm in diameter). Quarter and peel the apples, remove and discard the cores and cut the quarters lengthwise several times but do not slice. Press the apples quarters circularly into the dough with the curved side down. Brush the jelly on top.
Bake the cake in the pre-heated oven (bottom tray) for approx. 40 minutes. Place on a wire rack and leave to cool. Sprinkle with icing sugar before serving.

Butter cake

This is the party cake in north Germany. It is served at almost every festive event.

For the dough: 500 g flour, 1 sachet dried yeast,
2 tbsp sugar, 1 pinch of salt, 1/8 l lukewarm milk,
1 egg and 1 yolk (room temperature)
For the topping: 250 g butter, 200 g fine sugar,
1/4 tsp cinnamon, 1 sachet vanilla sugar,
250 g almonds slices, fat for the baking tray

To make the dough mix the flour, yeast, sugar and salt. Add the milk, egg and egg yolk. Stir for 10 minutes with a hand mixer using the dough hook. After this the dough should be bubbly and not stuck to the bowl. Cover and leave to rise in a warm place for 1 hour, by which time the dough should have doubled in volume. Shortly knead once again and spread out evenly in a fatted baking tray. Pre-heat the oven to 180 °C (fan-assisted oven 160 °C, gas 3). Make 7 cm offset indents in the dough, using the handle of a wooden spoon. Fill with small pieces of butter. Mix the sugar, cinnamon and vanilla sugar with the almonds and spread over the cake. Let rise for a 15 minutes. Bake the cake in the pre-warmed oven (middle tray) for approx. 25 minutes.

 For crumble cake topping knead 200 g cold butter with 200 g sugar. Add 300 g flour and 1 tsp cinnamon. Mix the ingredients together, crumble, spread evenly over the dough and bake as above.

Zwetschgendatschi – Plum cake

50 g butter, 300 g flour,
1/2 sachet dried yeast, 2 tbsp sugar,
a pinch of salt, 1/8 l lukewarm milk,
1 egg (room temperature), 2 kg ripe plums,
flour to roll out the dough,
fat for the baking tray, 2 tbsp breadcrumbs,
100 g caster sugar for sprinkling

Melt the butter and let it cool lukewarm. Mix the flour with the yeast, sugar and salt in bowl. Add 2 tbsp liquid butter, the milk and egg. Stir for 10 minutes with a hand mixer using the dough hook. By then the dough should be bubbly and not stuck to the bowl. Cover and leave to rise in a warm place for 1 hour, by then the dough should have doubled in volume. In the meantime wash, halve and stone the plums. Deep cut the halves but do not slice.
Knead the dough thoroughly on a floured working surface, roll out on a fatted baking tin and sprinkle with breadcrumbs. Press the plums shingle-style with the

skin side down into the dough. Leave covered, for a further 15 minutes. Pre-heat the oven to 200 °C (fan-assisted oven 180 °C, gas 3). Bake the cake for 35 minutes (middle tray). Brush the rest of the butter on the plums, sprinkle with sugar. Turn off the oven and return the cake to draw for a further 5 minutes. Take out and leave to settle on the tray for 20 minutes. Cut into pieces and place on a wire rack. Serve immediately or lukewarm.

 Use late plums, available from September, for this classic German cake. The plums should have an aromatic taste and just enough juice for the cake be juicy but not soggy. Use fine granulated sugar so that it melts well in the oven.

Marble cake

Birthdays, Sunday breakfasts and afternoon teas are three occasions when this cake is usually served. Wrapped in tin foil it tastes for days.

250 g soft butter, 200 g sugar,
1 tbsp vanilla sugar, 1 tsp untreated lemon peel,
a pinch of salt, 3 large eggs, 500 g flour,
1 sachet baking powder, approx. 1/8 l milk,
30 g unsweetened cocoa powder,
50 g peeled crushed almonds,
2 tbsp rum or milk,
fat for the baking tin,
icing sugar for sprinkling

Pre-heat the oven to 180 °C (fan-assisted oven 160 °C, gas 2). Cream the butter with sugar, vanilla sugar, lemon peel and the salt until light and fluffy. First add the eggs, then mix in a mixture of flour and baking powder in two or three portions. Add enough milk to allow all ingredients to become a creamy dough which easy drops off the stirring spoon. Fill two thirds of the dough in a well-fatted ring cake tin (24 cm in diameter). Mix the remaining dough with cocoa, almonds, rum or milk. Top the dough in the tin with this mixture. To achieve the marble effect draw spirals with a fork through both layers. Bake in the pre-warmed oven (lowest tray) for about 1 hour. Remove from the tin, place on a wire rack and leave to cool. When serving sprinkle with icing sugar.

Cheese cake

For the base: 250 g flour, 200 g butter,
100 sugar, 1 sachet vanilla sugar, 2 eggs,
1 pinch of salt, 1 pinch of cinnamon
For the topping: 100 g butter, 250 g sugar,
2 sachets vanilla sugar, 4 eggs, 80 g flour,
1/2 sachet vanilla pudding powder,
1 kg creamy curd
In addition: butter for the tin

For the base sieve the flour onto a working surface,
form a hole in the middle. Spread small pieces of butter, sugar and vanilla sugar around the edge. Add in
the eggs, salt and cinnamon. Quickly knead the ingredients from the middle to a smooth dough. Cool in
cling foil for 1 hour.
In the meantime for the topping cream the butter with
sugar and vanilla sugar until light and fluffy. Add the
eggs one by one. Add the flour and pudding powder
and mix well. Finally add the curd.
Pre-heat the oven to 200 °C, (fan-assisted oven 180 °C,
gas 3). Roll out the dough and fill the base of a fatted
loose-bottomed cake tin (26 cm in diameter) and form
a 2 cm rim. Add the curd mixture and bake light brown
in the pre-warmed oven (lowest tray) for 50 minutes.

 In many German households it is quite usual to
cover the base with well drained tinned mandarin
oranges, sour cherries or rum raisins before the
curd filling is added.

List of recipes

Soups and stews

Simple dishes to beer and wine

Fish dishes

Meat dishes

Vegetable, potato and noodle dishes

Desserts and cakes